The publishers' thanks to Lucile Seguin, bacteriologist, The City of New York Department of Hospitals, and to Dr. Charles Poser of the Neurological Institute of New York for their helpful suggestions concerning this book.

Illustrations on pages 15, 22, 26, 27, 28, 29, and 31 are adapted from *Animals Without Backbones* by Ralph Buchsbaum by permission of The University of Chicago Press. Copyright 1938 and 1948 by The University of Chicago. All rights reserved. Published November 1938. Second Edition 1948. Second Impression 1950. Composed and printed by The University of Chicago Press, Chicago, Illinois, U. S. A.

FOURTH PRINTING

Library of Congress Catalog Card Number: 55-7783

Printed in the United States of America by Polygraphic Company of America

THE FIRST BOOK OF
MICROBES

by LUCIA Z. LEWIS, Ph. D.
Department of Biology, Duquesne University

Pictures by MARGUERITE SCOTT

FRANKLIN WATTS, INC.
575 LEXINGTON AVENUE
NEW YORK 22, N.Y.

WHAT ARE MICROBES?

Microbes are living things—tiny plants and animals that grow almost everywhere in the world around you. At this very moment thousands of them are floating in the air before the pages of this book. Many more are clinging to its cover, to your hands, and to your clothes. You cannot see them because they are so small. Microbes are so tiny that 25,000 of one particular kind, placed end to end, would measure only one inch. A single

microbe can be seen only under a microscope, which makes it seem many times as big as it really is.

Scientists call these small plants and animals *micro-organisms* (MY-cro-OR-gan-isms), from the word "micro" meaning "small," and "organism," meaning a "living being." Almost everyone else calls them microbes (MY-crobes), a name that comes from two Greek words which, put together, mean "small life."

3

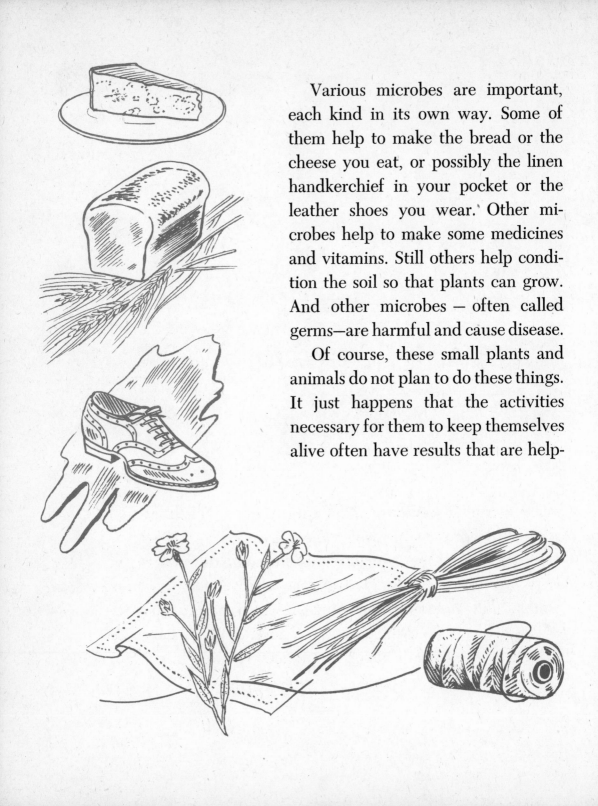

Various microbes are important, each kind in its own way. Some of them help to make the bread or the cheese you eat, or possibly the linen handkerchief in your pocket or the leather shoes you wear. Other microbes help to make some medicines and vitamins. Still others help condition the soil so that plants can grow. And other microbes — often called germs—are harmful and cause disease.

Of course, these small plants and animals do not plan to do these things. It just happens that the activities necessary for them to keep themselves alive often have results that are help-

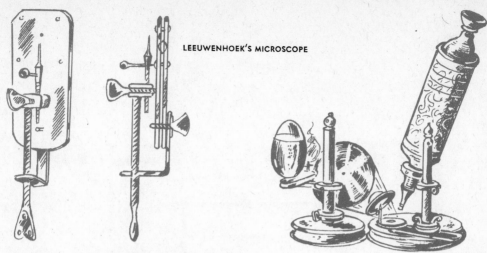
LEEUWENHOEK'S MICROSCOPE

ROBERT HOOKE'S MICROSCOPE

ful or harmful to other living things.

Most microbes are harmless, and many are very helpful. In fact, life on earth would be impossible without them. It is hard to believe, but human beings and all plants and animals, however large, depend partly on these unseen little bits of life for their existence.

The invisible world of microbes is a fascinating one, crowded with strange plants and animals living in odd ways and peculiar places. Scientists today, with the aid of microscopes, have been able to learn much about these tiny bits of life.

5

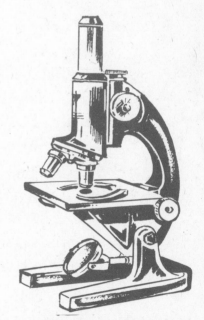
MODERN RESEARCH MICROSCOPE

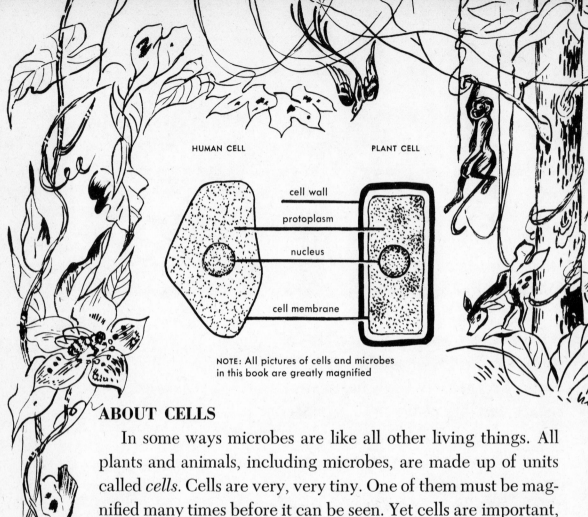

HUMAN CELL

PLANT CELL

cell wall

protoplasm

nucleus

cell membrane

NOTE: All pictures of cells and microbes
in this book are greatly magnified

ABOUT CELLS

In some ways microbes are like all other living things. All plants and animals, including microbes, are made up of units called *cells*. Cells are very, very tiny. One of them must be magnified many times before it can be seen. Yet cells are important, for they are the building blocks of life. Just as bricks cemented together can build houses and walls, so millions of cells joined together can form many different living things. Cells make a tree, a dog, a flower, and even you. Cells make microbes, too. Most microbes are one-piece plants and animals, however; each of them has only a single cell.

Whether cells form the biggest elephant or the tiniest bug, the tallest tree or the shortest blade of grass—or the smallest microbe that lives—their basic parts are much the same.

Cells are usually oval in shape. Some of them, however, have other shapes—some long and thin, some almost cubical, and others many-sided. A thin outside layer, called a *membrane*, encloses each of them. Most plant cells are also enclosed by a thicker wall on top of the membrane. Sometimes this wall is stiff, and helps make the plant tough and somewhat rigid.

Inside the cell's membrane is a clear sticky liquid called *protoplasm* (PRO-to-plazm). This is the fluid that somehow makes the cell *alive*. As yet scientists do not know how. They know that protoplasm is made up of many different chemicals mixed together with water. They can break down a cell and find out what chemicals it contains. But when they mix these same chemicals together they cannot make living protoplasm. What makes this liquid *alive* is one of the great mysteries of science.

The chemical parts of protoplasm vary in proportion in different kinds of cells. The protoplasm of fish, for example, does not have the same chemical make-up as the protoplasm of flowers or birds or anything else.

In most living cells, protoplasm is divided into two main parts. Most of the cell is filled with a rather thin jelly-like substance. In the center of this substance, in most cells, is a small,

7

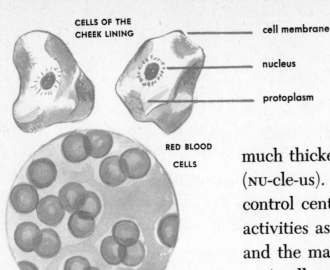

CELLS OF THE
CHEEK LINING

cell membrane

nucleus

protoplasm

RED BLOOD
CELLS

much thicker spot called the *nucleus* (NU-cle-us). This nucleus is the cell's control center. It regulates such cell activities as growth, the use of food, and the making of various products.

A cell must do many things in order to keep alive. It must get food for nourishment. It must take in some gas, usually oxygen, to help make energy. It must be able to grow. And finally it must be able to make other cells like itself. In a body built of many cells, like yours, certain cells have some special functions, also. The cells of your skin, for example, form a tough protective covering for your body. Your tongue has certain cells by means of which you can tell whether the food you eat is sweet, salt, acid, or bitter.

The cells in the root tips of a green plant must take in certain minerals and water from the soil so that the plant can make food. Leaf cells must take in gas from the air and give off waste gases to the air.

In microbes the various activities are not divided. Each cell, which is usually one microbe, is a complete unit for living, able to carry on all the activities necessary for the microbe's existence.

8

DISCOVERING MICROBES

Microbes are perhaps the strangest of all living things. Ordinarily you have no trouble in telling a plant from an animal. You know, for instance, that a rosebush is a plant and that a rabbit is an animal. Of course, that's easy! But many microbes are so small and so peculiar that it is sometimes hard to tell whether a particular one is a plant or an animal. Among these one-celled microbes are plants that are not green, have no roots to anchor them to the ground, and have no stems, leaves, or flowers. Some of these plant microbes can even move around. The animal microbes are just as queer. They have no stomachs, and most of them have no mouths. They have no legs or tails, no eyes or hair or any other features that you consider a part of the usual animal. Only after long study have scientists been able to classify each microbe as a plant or an animal, according to its particular way of living.

Microbes have lived on earth for a long, long time. Rocks from prehistoric ages show evidence of them. It was not until a few centuries ago, however, that anyone really thought much about them. In fact, until then no one knew of the existence of some of the smallest ones. In 1683 a Dutchman named Anton van Leeuwenhoek (vahn LAY-ven-hook) saw, probably for the first time, some of the microbes that scientists today call *bacteria*. He was the first man to draw pictures of actual bacteria.

Leeuwenhoek was a strange man. For a time he worked in a merchant's office in Amsterdam. But he spent his spare time grinding magnifying lenses so that he might see what tiny un-dreamed-of things could be found on common objects. Soon

10

he began manufacturing simple microscopes. He peered at everything through his microscopes—at sewage, rain water, and pepper soup. He even stopped people on the street and asked them for their saliva so that he might see what was in it. Leeuwenhoek was not a scientist, but he was a very careful observer. He accurately described all the strange things he saw through his lenses. One day he discovered tiny wriggling creatures swimming around in a drop of water. He called them "tiny animalcules" and "wretched beasties." He wrote long letters to the learned members of the Royal Society in London. In them he told of his unusual discoveries and drew pictures of his "beasties." Scientists today recognize the bacteria he drew and say that his pictures are excellent.

Since Leeuwenhoek's time scientists have improved on his crude lenses until they have developed a much more powerful microscope. Inside it are lenses which enlarge things as much as a thousand times.

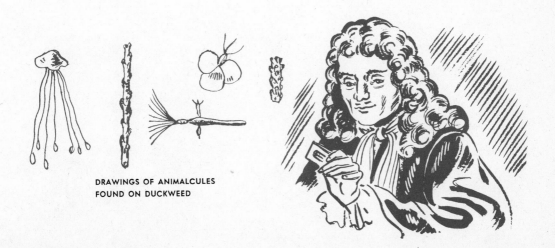

DRAWINGS OF ANIMALCULES
FOUND ON DUCKWEED

For a long time after people knew that microbes existed almost no one connected them with such everyday happenings as fermentation, cheese making, and food spoilage. In fact, it was not until the 1800's that a famous Frenchman named Louis Pasteur (Pahs-TURR) definitely showed how microbes cause the change called fermentation.

Pasteur put portions of broth into flasks. When the broth became rancid he looked at it through a microscope. It was swarming with microbes. When he boiled more broth and sealed it at once, it stayed fresh and contained no microbes. Where did they come from? He suspected they were carried through the air.

Next Pasteur boiled yeast broth in glass flasks, heated the flasks' necks, and bent them in deep double curves. Soup boiled in these flasks never spoiled, even when the flasks were left unsealed. Pasteur figured out the reasons. First, microbes in the broth were killed by the heat of boiling; and second, mi-

LOUIS PASTEUR

12

crobes from the air could not reach the broth because they could not go around the curves in the flasks' necks.

Pasteur discovered many other things about microbes. He found how, by vaccination, cattle and sheep could be protected against a terrible disease called anthrax—a disease caused by microbes. He saved the silk industry of France by finding the microbes that were causing disease among the silkworms, and by suggesting ways of fighting them. While working for France's wine industry he found that microbes change grape juice into wine. Pasteur showed that certain microbes in the vats made the wine bitter and foul-smelling, while other microbes produced fine sweet wine. He developed a method of heating the wine, then cooling it rapidly to kill the harmful microbes. Today this process is called pasteurization, in honor of this famous Frenchman Pasteur. In this country, pasteurization is used chiefly to kill harmful microbes in milk and make it safe to drink.

Since Pasteur's day, scientists have made many important discoveries about microbes. They have learned about the various species, where they live, and what they do. They have learned how to grow microbes, how to kill them, how to control many of them, and how to make use of others. Every day new discoveries are being made about these tiny plants and animals.

13

SMALL BUT NUMEROUS

All microbes have one thing in common: their very small size. It is hard to realize just how tiny microbes are. Imagine the smallest thing you have ever seen: a grain of very fine sand, the tip of a needle, a particle of dust. One microbe is about one thousand times smaller than any of these. Look at one single hair on your head. Notice how thin it is. Sixty microbes lying side by side would fill a space as wide as that hair. And remember, 25,000 of one kind of microbe lined up end to end measure one inch!

Microbes may be the smallest living creatures on earth, but they are also the most numerous. There are more microbes on earth than there are fish in the oceans or ants in the anthills. The microbe family is very complex, with thousands of types, or *species,* as they are called. Each species has its own definite shape and build, its particular kind of food and living surroundings. And each thrives best in a particular climate.

Scientists have given each of these species a name consisting of two parts—usually in Greek or Latin. The first part tells what group, or *genus,* each microbe belongs to, and the second part tells its particular species. Together, the names often describe something about the plant or animal. For instance, the microbes which are named *Volvox perglobator* are so called because of these facts about them: They form into colonies like

14

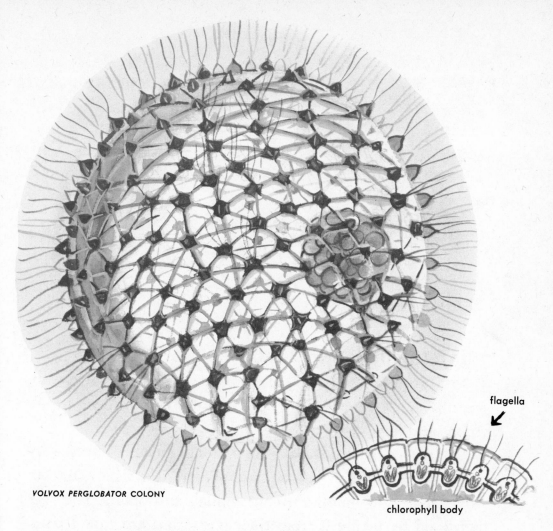

VOLVOX PERGLOBATOR COLONY

flagella

chlorophyll body

round balls, which swim through the water by rolling over and over. *Volvox* comes from a Latin word meaning "to roll." *Perglobator* means "globelike." Names like these are valuable to scientists as a way of indicating microbes quickly without a great deal of written explanation.

15

WHAT MICROBES NEED FOR LIVING

Just as human beings must have food, water, oxygen, warmth, and various other things in order to stay alive, so microbes also have certain needs.

Of course they must have food. Some microbes need very rich food. Others can live on simple materials. There are microbes that grow on other *living* animals and plants. They get their food by taking it from their hosts, and are called *parasites* (PAR-a-sites). Microbes that cause disease are usually parasites.

Other microbes get their food from *non-living* things such as dead animals and old tree stumps and other dead plants. They are the microbes of decay. Scientists call them *saprophytes*

16

(SAP-ro-fites). When a plant or animal dies these microbes go to work, using up the material in its cells. You have seen this happen many times. Think of the leaves that drop from plants each autumn. They turn brown and gradually fall apart until they are only a powder. Microbes are getting food from these leaves—breaking them down until very little is left. Most microbes are saprophytes. They make up more than 95 per cent of the microbe family.

Microbes need water, too. Water is just as important to the smallest one-celled plant or animal as it is to you. Microbes use it to help build new protoplasm and digest food, and for every life activity. Without water most microbes gradually shrink up and many of them die.

17

Each kind of microbe has a special temperature at which it grows best. This temperature is not the same for every species of microbe. Some can live where it is cold. There are microbes growing in the arctic ice and snow. Other microbes live where it is quite warm—in the tropics and in hot springs. Most microbes, however, grow best in mild temperatures: at just about the warmth of your body or perhaps of a nice summer day. That is why foods spoil and decay more quickly in summertime—why it is especially important to refrigerate them in hot weather.

All microbes breathe, though not with lungs as you do. But they all take some gas, or air, into their bodies. It merely passes through their outside layer. Inside the cell the gas works together with the microbes' food to make energy. Energy is just as important for a microbe as it is for you. It gives the microbe power to get more food, to build new protoplasm, to carry on all activities. Most microbes take in oxygen, the same gas you breathe. Waste gas, such as carbon dioxide, passes back through the outside layer.

A few microbes will not grow with oxygen. These non-oxygen-using kinds need some other gas such as nitrogen for making energy. In nature they are usually found buried in the soil, under piles of junk, or deep in animal cells—in places where large amounts of oxygen do not enter.

Most microbes grow best in darkness. Direct sunlight is very

18

harmful to many kinds and often kills them. Sunlight is a natural control which keeps down the number of microbes.

Food, water, favorable temperature, gas for breathing, and sometimes darkness—these are the microbes' most important needs for living and growing. If one of them is taken away, these microscopic plants and animals may not be able to survive.

You can grow microbes in your own home. It's very easy. Put a little meat broth in a cup and allow it to stand near a heater overnight. By morning or soon after you will find that the broth has become cloudy and smells bad. Microbes from the air have fallen into it and have started to use it as food. You say the soup is spoiled. Really it is starting to decay. A microscope would show that it is swarming with microbes.

Another way to grow microbes is to moisten a piece of bread with water and put it in a warm dark place. In a few days a fuzzy grayish growth—mold—will cover the bread like a fine web. A few days later tiny black specks will appear. Finally the whole piece of bread will become black. The bread itself will fall apart and will have a bad odor. Mold microbes and bacteria are gradually consuming it.

Scientists often grow microbes in laboratories in order to study their forms, to learn how they live and develop, and to discover the many things they do. To grow these microbes, the scientists make a special food—a sort of broth—which they put

into carefully sterilized tubes. In the tubes they also place a few of the species of microbes they are studying. Sometimes they add sugar, salt, gelatin, and even blood to help the microbes grow. Then they plug the tubes with cotton, which acts as a filter. It keeps microbes in the air from entering the tubes, and prevents microbes in the tubes from escaping. Air, however, can pass through the cotton so that the microbes in the tubes can breathe. The tubes are then stored in the proper gas and temperature, in dark closets called incubators. Within a short time enough of the microbes have grown so that the scientists can watch them through their microscopes and experiment with them.

MICROBES AND THEIR FOOD

Microbes have no teeth for chewing, and most of them have no mouths. They have no stomachs or intestines for digesting food. How then, you may ask, do these microscopic plants and animals get nourishment?

Some plant microbes make their food as green plants do from air, water, and minerals, with the help of a green substance called *chlorophyll* (KLO-ro-fil). Most plant microbes, however, take food into their bodies in liquid form. Some of them simply absorb what they need from their surroundings. Others give off special chemicals which break down solid food around them into a fluid that can pass through their outer membrane. Any waste material—gases or water—can pass out through the membrane. This outer membrane is a little bit like a sieve with

21

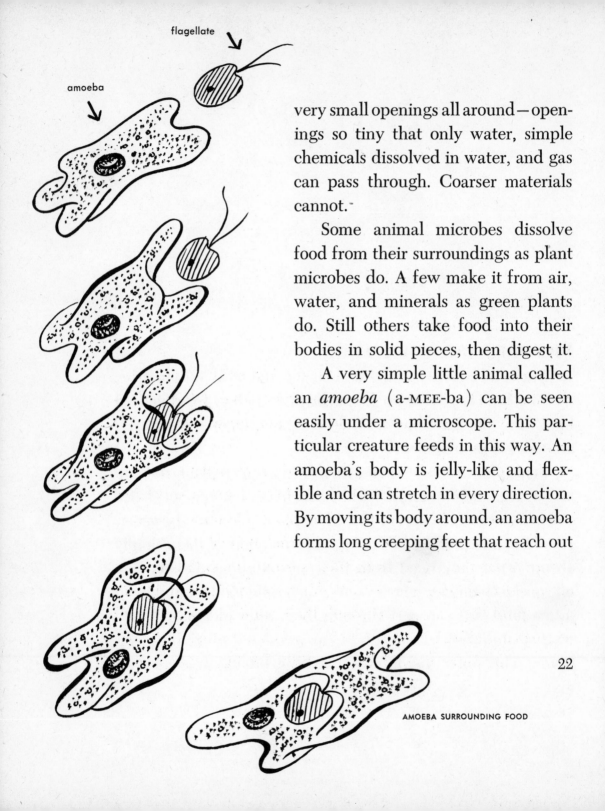

flagellate

amoeba

very small openings all around—openings so tiny that only water, simple chemicals dissolved in water, and gas can pass through. Coarser materials cannot.

Some animal microbes dissolve food from their surroundings as plant microbes do. A few make it from air, water, and minerals as green plants do. Still others take food into their bodies in solid pieces, then digest it.

A very simple little animal called an *amoeba* (a-MEE-ba) can be seen easily under a microscope. This particular creature feeds in this way. An amoeba's body is jelly-like and flexible and can stretch in every direction. By moving its body around, an amoeba forms long creeping feet that reach out

22

AMOEBA SURROUNDING FOOD

very slowly. Sooner or later one of these feet accidentally bumps into a piece of food—probably another microbe. Gradually the foot surrounds this until the food is inside the amoeba's body. There the piece of food moves around and around while digestive chemicals work on it. Gradually it is broken down into simpler products. The animal then uses these products for making new protoplasm, creating energy, and for all its other life activities.

If the amoeba does not need at that time all the food it has taken in, the surplus is stored away in spaces called *vacuoles* (VACK-u-oles). When the amoeba cannot find food outside, it uses that from its vacuoles.

The amoeba gets rid of waste products very easily. After it has digested every bit of food that it can, the waste products collect inside its body in very tiny pieces. These wastes are moved around until they reach the thin outer membrane. Then they are pushed out through this membrane as the amoeba moves along.

So these tiny animals, so small you cannot see them, capture food, digest it, and even store it away for emergencies.

Most plant microbes do not have special food-storage spaces, although a few of them do store bits of iron and sulfur in their bodies.

23

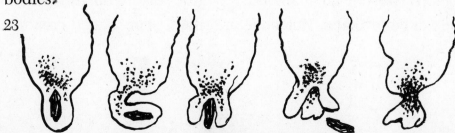

WASTE PRODUCTS PUSHING THROUGH MEMBRANE

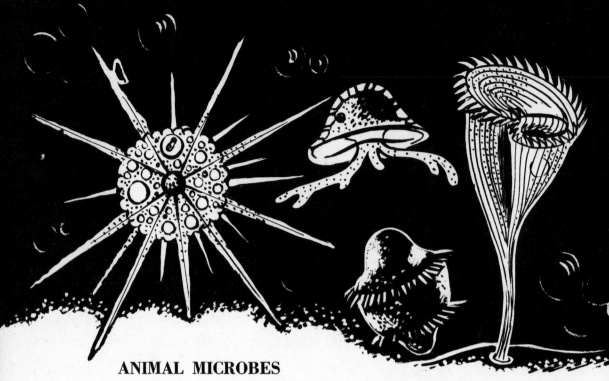

ANIMAL MICROBES

Animal microbes belong to a special group called *protozoa* (pro-to-zo-a), almost all of which are one-celled creatures. The protozoa family is a large and peculiar one. Some of the varieties differ so greatly from one another that it is hard to believe that they belong to the same family.

Some protozoa live in damp soil or in the bodies of human beings and animals. Most of these small animals, however, live in water. A microscope shows hundreds of these wriggling creatures swimming about in a single drop of pond water. They are queer-looking animals—probably not like any you have seen before. Most of them are just tiny globs of protoplasm without any definite shape. But some are small cigar-shaped creatures

that dash crazily about. Others look like little horns or weird false faces. There are various other forms, too.

Protozoa are the smallest and simplest animals that live. A view through a microscope shows the way most of them are built. They have a definite nucleus in the center, and little food-storage spaces scattered throughout their single cell. Some even have special mouth parts through which food can pass.

Most protozoa can move about freely. The way in which they do this is one means by which scientists tell them apart. Since so many of them live in water they move chiefly by swimming as they wriggle about searching for food or trying to escape harm.

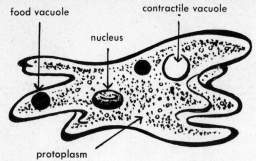

food vacuole

contractile vacuole

nucleus

← false foot

protoplasm

The members of one group of protozoa move by pushing their bodies out in many directions. They form long oozing props that are called *false feet*. As the false feet reach out, the whole microbe moves with them. The amoeba is a member of this group. If you were to watch its stretchy body under a microscope you might think it was made of rubber. This simple animal moves very, very slowly—so slowly that it would take many days to travel a few inches.

An amoeba has such a thin outer membrane that its body is actually transparent. If the water in its pond dries up or freezes, an amoeba protects itself by curling into a little ball with a hard protective covering. This hard ball, called a cyst (sist), is very tough and can live for a long time under very bad conditions. When the emergency is over, the amoeba comes out of its cyst and starts active life again.

Amoebas consume other animal microbes, some plant microbes, and some bits of dead plant or animal matter. They have no mouths and can take in food at any place, simply by encircling it as was described on page 22. Because of their food habits they help clean up streams and ponds. Amoebas also furnish food for baby fish. Without these tiny microbes to feed upon, some kinds of young fish might not live.

A second group of protozoa move by means of a long thread or threads which are attached to their outer membranes. These thin threads are like whips. In fact, scientists call them *flagella* (fla-JEL-la), a Latin word meaning "whip." By whipping and lashing their flagella back and forth the microbes can move themselves through water. Flagella are their outboard motors.

Many of the protozoa use these little whip-hairs for capturing food, also. When a piece of food comes near, out stretches a thread and captures it. Then the food is pushed into a tiny opening or mouth near the base of the flagella. After it has passed through this opening it enters the cell and is digested. Extra food is stored away inside the cell. Waste products are passed out through the mouth or pushed out of a little opening on the side.

A few of the microbes with flagella are dangerous, as they can enter a human or animal body and cause disease. Most of them, however, are harmless. Some are even useful. Some termites—those small insects that eat wood—have in their stomachs microbes with flagella. These little animals break down the tough wood fibers the termites have eaten. The termites themselves are unable to digest wood. They would starve to death if there were no microbes in their stomachs to do this for them.

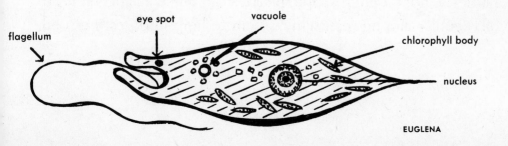

flagellum   eye spot   vacuole   chlorophyll body   nucleus

EUGLENA

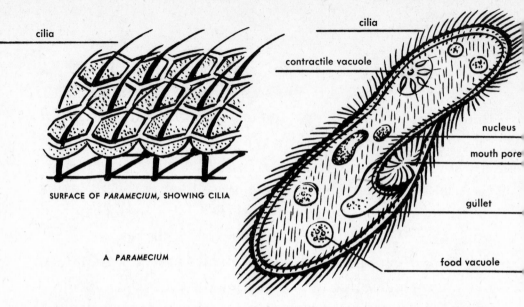

cilia

cilia

contractile vacuole

nucleus

mouth pore

gullet

food vacuole

SURFACE OF *PARAMECIUM*, SHOWING CILIA

A *PARAMECIUM*

A third type of protozoa move by means of short hairs which cover each animal. These hairlike bristles are called *cilia* (SILL-i-a). The microbes swim by beating the cilia back and forth. The short hairs bend, then straighten together like oars on a boat and push the microbes through the water.

Most of these microbes with cilia take in food through a small mouthlike opening about halfway down the side of the body. Around this mouth are stronger cilia which help the animal capture food and push it into the opening. From the mouth, the food passes into the cell where it is digested. Storage places are formed, and waste materials are usually pushed out through the membrane. These microbes have many parts inside their bodies. Under a microscope, besides the nucleus, special types of vacuoles can be seen which seem to help in digesting food.

CILIA IN MOTION

Most microbes with cilia are harmless. Many of them have strange and interesting shapes. The slipper-shaped *Paramecium* is an interesting one to watch. It can be found in almost any drop of pond water. Under a microscope it looks like a whirling top as it darts back and forth and turns over and over almost faster than the eye can travel.

A SAMPLING OF POND WATER, MAGNIFIED GREATLY

Another group of protozoa have no special structures such as whiplike threads to help them move. They are all parasites that live in human beings and other kinds of animal life. Many of these protozoa are harmful. Among them are the microbes that cause malaria. The life of the malaria microbe is a complicated one. Part of it is spent in the blood stream of a human being and part in a certain kind of mosquito called *Anopheles* (a-NOF-a-leez), found particularly in warm regions. This is what happens. The microbes that cause malaria develop to a certain stage in the stomach of a malaria mosquito. At that stage they move to the glands surrounding the sucking tube of the insect. Then, if the mosquito bites a person, the microbes enter the person's body in the mosquito's saliva. In the human body they start multiplying very rapidly in the red blood cells. When they fill these cells they cause them to burst. Then the person has the chills and fever of malaria. Finally, when some of the microbes reach another stage, they are taken into the stomach of any malaria mosquito that bites the person. There they undergo more stages in their development. Then the whole life story starts over again—mosquito to human being, human being to mosquito, and so on. Both the body of a human being and that of a malaria mosquito are absolutely necessary to this particular microbe if it is to go on living.

Many protozoa have much simpler lives than this, however.

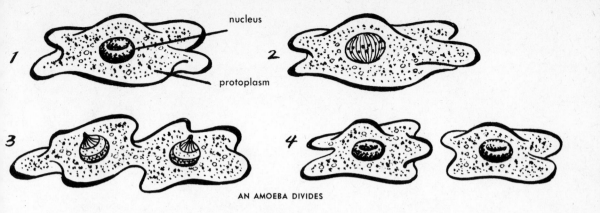

nucleus

protoplasm

AN AMOEBA DIVIDES

They form new protozoa simply by splitting in two. When they are ready to divide, tiny particles in the nucleus start moving around. Gradually they line up equally on either side of the nucleus, like two teams ready to play tug of war. Then a tiny break starts in the middle of the nucleus just as if the teams were pulling away from each other. They pull and pull until the nucleus breaks in half. Now there are two nuclei. (Nuclei is the name given more than one nucleus.) These nuclei move to opposite ends of the cell and force the cell itself to split in half. Now there are two protozoa, each one complete and free to grow. In time they will split and make two more protozoa, which in turn will split and form other protozoa, and so on.

The family of protozoa is a large one. Not all of its members are harmful. Often, however, because of the damage some protozoa do, many people forget the helpfulness of others of the group. Most protozoa are useful microbes, important to all of us.

31

ALGAE

Some plant microbes belong to the *algae* (AL-jee) group, which has some members that live as single cells. Small as these are, many of them contain the same green matter, chlorophyll, which colors the leaves of many of our familiar large plants. Because these small algae have chlorophyll they are able to make their own food as other green plants do. With the aid of light and chlorophyll they combine the gas, carbon dioxide, and water to make sugar, their food. They do not thrive in strong sunlight, however, but grow best in shady spots. Some of the algae, although they contain green chlorophyll, are brown or red in color.

Algae grow in the water or where there is a great deal of moisture. They can exist alone as free one-celled plants or they can join together to form very large growths. The green scum that grows on quiet ponds in the woods is a type of algae. So are

32

the green mossy coats growing on the north side of tree trunks, covering the soil in moist shady spots, and clinging to damp rocks and flower pots. Woodsmen often look for the algae on tree trunks to point out the northerly direction and so guide them through the wilderness.

Large groups of algae growing together form lovely water weeds in lakes and oceans. Home aquarium owners usually put some of these green water weeds in their tanks to help keep the water fresh.

Algae are important to water life. They give off oxygen, which helps freshen the surrounding water. Some of them furnish food for fish. Algae are also important because they are rich in many minerals, especially iodine. In some countries, some of the algae that grow as seaweeds are used as food, and others are used as fertilizers for the soil.

33

MOLDS

Molds and mildews are plant microbes almost everyone knows. You have probably seen bread spotted with black fuzz, or old lemons covered with a greenish growth. Or possibly you have found black mildew spots on clothes that have been stored for a long time in a damp place. These growths are *fungi* (FUN-ji), members of the fungus family. Many fungi are so small that they do not show clearly except under a microscope. The reason you can see molds and mildews so easily on bread or elsewhere is that many hundreds of microbes are joined together to form large colonies.

Fungi have no chlorophyll and cannot make their own food. They usually live on dead materials. A few fungi, however, are parasites and grow on living things. For example, ringworm and athlete's foot, two skin diseases of human beings, are caused by fungus growths.

Molds are strange microbes. The black fuzzy growth from moldy bread looks like a tangled spider web when it is viewed through a microscope. It started as one tiny spot so small that only a microscope could detect it. Soon it grew to a thread, which became longer and longer and branched many times. Finally its dense network of many fuzzy threads was built up. These threads grow every which way—some down into the bread and some along its surface.

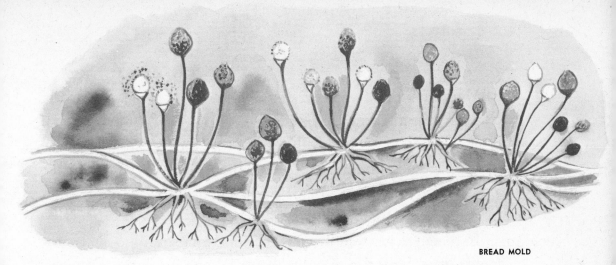

Molds grow very quickly. When they first start, they form a soft white fuzzy film. Gradually, as the mold grows older, the web becomes denser and coarser and changes color. Then, when the mold is ready to produce new plants, little stalks are sent up from the network. Upon these are the sacs, or holders, for tiny seedlike bodies called spores. The black spots on a piece of moldy bread are its spore sacs. Each of them holds many spores. When these spores are ripe the sacs break open and the spores fall out. Wind, insects, animals, or even the faintest current of air spreads them far and wide. If a spore happens to fall in a suitable spot, a whole new mold network will develop.

Molds grow in a great variety of places. They do not need sunlight, but they do need moisture. You may find them on damp cellar walls, old leather shoes, and moist clothing. They grow easily on jellies and other food and cause a great deal of food spoilage.

35

Many molds, however, have been put to useful work. Cheeses are aged by letting molds grow over them. Special types of molds are carefully added to some cheeses such as Roquefort and Camembert to give them their particular flavor and smell. Those bluish-black streaks in crumbly white Roquefort cheese are the mold growing in it.

In recent years scientists have found an exciting new use for molds in making the wonder drugs known an *antibiotics* (AN-ti-by-OTT-iks). Penicillin, which is used in treating many kinds of infection, is one of these drugs. It and most of the other antibiotics are made from chemicals given off by molds as they grow.

Alexander Fleming, an Englishman, discovered penicillin in 1929. Quite by accident the tiny spore of a certain blue-green mold had landed in a dish of disease microbes with which he was experimenting in his laboratory. The mold started to grow, and Fleming noticed that all around it in a ring his disease microbes were dead! This started him thinking and wondering if possibly the mold might be useful in fighting disease. He grew more of it and made from it a broth which he injected into mice with various infections. Sure enough, his mysterious broth seemed to kill some kinds of disease microbes.

For some years scientists did not pay much attention to Fleming's discoveries. But later more work was done and the

PENICILLIN CRYSTALS

great importance of penicillin was realized. Today it is produced in giant vats by large drug companies, and doctors everywhere use it in fighting some kinds of disease microbes. Its discovery opened the door to a whole new variety of drugs, the antibiotics: terramycin, streptomycin and others.

Many lives have been saved by antibiotics, and scientists are constantly experimenting, hoping to find more molds that can be used in making them. The blue-green mold from which penicillin is produced is a common one, often found growing on old fruit. Terramycin comes from a microbe of the soil. Many molds are of no use in making antibiotics, but there is always the chance of discovering one whose chemical products can mysteriously kill disease microbes.

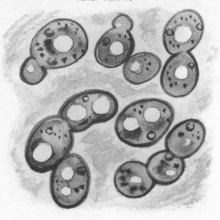

YEASTS

You may have seen yeast cakes, the small squares of yeast for breadmaking which may be bought at grocery stores. Did you know that in each of these little cakes are millions of living one-celled plants? It is true that a pasty white yeast cake does not look like a plant. If a piece is broken off, mixed in a little water, and viewed through a microscope, however, it appears as a group of very strange little plant microbes.

There are various kinds of yeasts—all very simple plants, almost always oval in shape. They have no color and usually grow as small separate cells, although some may be joined together in chains. Yeasts are the largest plant microbes, but they still cannot be seen unless they are magnified many times by a microscope.

They grow very quickly. A yeast plant usually develops completely in about thirty minutes. Then it starts to form new cells—usually in a peculiar way called budding. As a yeast cell grows, a small bump called a bud starts to form on its side. The bud grows larger and larger until it is so large that it becomes another cell. Now there are two yeast cells which may stay joined together but can easily break apart. In another thirty

38

minutes or so these form more cells, and so on, as the yeast grows and spreads. Sometimes, if a yeast cell is very active, it can form four or five buds at one time.

Yeast plants use a great deal of food. In an hour some of them take in more than their own weight in certain kinds of sugars. Within their cells they break down these sugars into simpler products: carbon dioxide—a gas—and alcohol. These products then pass out through the cell walls into the material surrounding the yeast.

The process of breaking down sugar into alcohol and carbon dioxide is called fermentation. Many important products are made by natural fermentation. Yeasts ferment grape juice to make wine. Under correct conditions they ferment grains to make beer, and sugars to form glycerine, a chemical with a great many uses.

Tiny yeast plants are almost everywhere around us, so fermentation is constantly going on. It causes the "spoiling" of many liquids containing sugars.

Yeast is very important in breadmaking, for it raises the bread. Bread dough is a mixture of flour, milk, sugar, butter, and salt. To this a cake of yeast is added. Then the dough is covered and allowed to stand in a warm place. As the yeast cells in the mixture become warm, they begin to grow and to absorb the sugar in the dough. Then, of course, fermentation starts. The sugar is broken down and alcohol and carbon dioxide gas are formed. The cells give off these products into the surrounding dough. Because the dough is so thick and sticky the gas cannot escape into the outside atmosphere, but is trapped in little pockets. As more gas is formed, these pockets swell and swell and so force the dough to puff up. This makes the bread light and fluffy and full of little holes which become even larger when the dough is baked. The alcohol given off by the yeast disappears during baking.

Not all yeasts are useful. Certain of them can cause disease. Some wild yeasts that grow on fruit can spoil the wine made from it. Industries using yeasts must be careful that no wild yeasts mix with the ones they grow especially for their manufacturing needs. Wild yeasts would make a product of a far different quality from the industry's usual one.

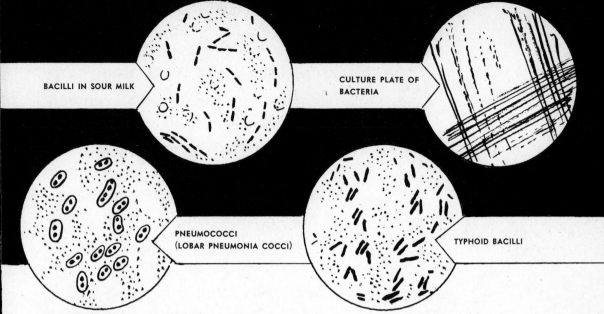

BACILLI IN SOUR MILK

CULTURE PLATE OF BACTERIA

PNEUMOCOCCI
(LOBAR PNEUMONIA COCCI)

TYPHOID BACILLI

BACTERIA

Smaller than yeasts are some of the tiny one-celled plants belonging to the group called *bacteria* (back-TEER-i-a). Bacteria have no leaves, roots, or stems. They are the simplest in form of all the microbes and have no definite nucleus. But, small and simple as they are, each one is an independent living cell that carries on many activities.

The bacteria family is a large one with hundreds of different species. These species differ in their food, living conditions, and activities, but in spite of their number and variety they grow in only three shapes. They are round, rodlike, or spiral— somewhat like a corkscrew.

Round bacteria are called *cocci* (KOK-seye), from a Greek word meaning "grain" or "seed." They are small masses of

41

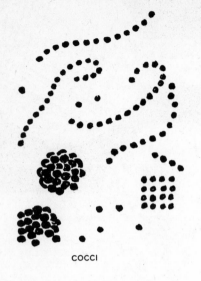

COCCI

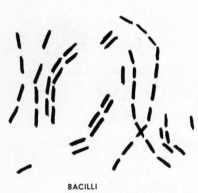

BACILLI

SPIRILLA

protoplasm shaped like balls. Sometimes these round bacteria grow in pairs, like twin balls stuck together. At other times they arrange themselves in long chains that look like strings of tiny beads. Still other round bacteria grow in clusters that resemble little bunches of grapes. These round bacteria float in the air at all times and are the causes of many infections.

Rod-shaped bacteria are called *bacilli* (ba-SILL-eye), from the Latin word meaning "little stick." Bacilli may be long or short, slender or quite fat, straight or slightly bent. Some may even branch to form little Y or V shapes. They look somewhat like stiff, very, very small tree twigs.

Some of these rod-shaped bacteria can move about. Several kinds have threadlike flagella by means of which they swim in liquid. Their flagella are usually very long—possibly four or five times longer than the microbe itself.

42

Some bacilli have only one thread, usually at one end. Others may have a thread at either end. Some have clusters of flagella. And others have little whiplike threads all around the cell.

The idea of plants moving about freely seems strange, as those we see most often are anchored firmly to the ground with roots. But bacilli are plants without roots to hold them, so they are free to travel. They live almost everywhere: in the soil, in water, floating on pieces of dust in the air. They can live in the mouths of human beings, in their intestines, and all over their bodies.

Spiral-shaped bacteria are called *spirilla* (spy-RILL-a), from the Latin word meaning "little coil." They may have very tightly coiled bodies or very loose spirals. Or some are merely shaped like little commas. The little corkscrew-shaped microbes are interesting to watch under a microscope. They whirl around like tops and because of their shape can bore through some materials. Most spirilla are harmless microbes. A few, however, can cause disease.

Bacteria have a very simple way of reproducing. When they reach a certain size they merely

43

SPIRILLA

split in half. Then there are two cells. Some bacteria can do this about once every twenty minutes. In a single day one of these can make many more like itself. Just imagine that you started with one bacillus. In twenty minutes there would be two, in forty minutes, four. In an hour there would be eight, then sixteen, thirty-two, sixty-four in only two hours. At the end of twenty-four hours there would be millions! Usually, however, before they reach the millions mark they have used up the food in their particular surroundings and have stopped reproducing.

One single microbe of the bacteria group is called a *bacterium*. When a bacterium falls in a favorable spot it takes in food and reproduces very quickly. Soon a whole family of bacteria develops—each one the same. If these bacteria happen to be growing on solid food, all of the microbes grow in a very tight cluster. Scientists say that these tight masses of bacteria have formed *colonies*. Colonies can be seen very easily without a microscope. The tiny spots growing on the surface of decayed food are often colonies of microbes. The spots may be red, yellow, white, gray, or black in color. They may be large and spreading, with ridges and curled edges, or they may be smooth shiny little circles. Some colonies are slimy, sticky droplets that ooze all over the surface of the food. Colonies are very interesting because they can be seen so easily and because they have so many unusual shapes and colors.

44

Scientists study the sizes and shapes of colonies for help in identifying the different species of bacteria.

Bacteria have various ways of protecting themselves. Some can surround themselves with a gummy coating, or capsule, which acts as a shield. This keeps the microbe inside safe, as the capsule is difficult to pierce.

Other bacteria shrink into little balls and build strong walls around themselves for protection against drying, strong heat, damaging chemicals, and sunlight. Even when they have no food or water, these microbes can stay alive for long periods inside of their walls. When living conditions become better, the walls break and the bacteria push out again.

VIRUSES

Among the microbes is another group called viruses. Most viruses are much smaller than the tiniest bacterium. They are so small, in fact, that they cannot be seen with an ordinary microscope. There is much still to be learned about these minute microbes, and scientists are constantly studying them. So far they know only of harmful ones that cause disease. Viruses are parasites which multiply only in the living cells of plants, animals, man, or even of other microbes. Everyone has probably been a host to these tiny microbes at some time. Among other diseases, they cause mumps, measles, and chicken pox.

FOR PLANTS TO GROW

Good fertile soil is important to everyone. Without it, plants could not grow. And without plants nothing else could live. For every living thing depends upon plants for food. It is true that some animals eat other animals. But those other animals may be plant-eaters, or they may, in turn, have as their food animals that are plant-eaters. At some point all living creatures, including people, depend on plants for food to live. And because they depend on plants they also depend on microbes. For microbes keep the soil supplied with the chemicals plants need for growing. There are many millions of microbes in each

square foot of earth. In the process of living their natural lives many kinds help make the soil rich.

Microbes help the farmer in several ways. First of all, they cause decay and so clear away dead matter. Think how terrible the world would be if all the plants and animals that die never disappeared but piled up year after year. In a short time there would be no green fields or clear streams, no bright-colored flowers or sweet-smelling forests. The earth would be hidden under a thick cloak of filth and dead things. Certain microbes prevent this from happening. This is one of the most important ways in which microbes help us.

47

After a plant withers, a leaf falls from a tree, an insect, an animal, or any other living thing dies, microbes attack it. Not all kinds of microbes do this at once, because not all of them use the same kinds of food. Rather, the microbes work in relays. In the process of getting food, one kind of microbe breaks down the dead material into simpler substances. Then another kind of microbe which can use these substances takes over, changing them into even simpler forms. And so it goes, with many kinds of microbes gradually changing the dead material until only simple chemicals, gases, water, and the humus of the soil are left. Not a bit of these is wasted. Each tiny particle becomes part of the soil or air.

Of the gases, carbon dioxide and ammonia are especially important to green plants. The plants must have carbon dioxide, much of which goes into the air, because it is one of the raw materials from which they make their food. And ammonia contains nitrogen, which plants must also have if they are to live. But most plants cannot use nitrogen as a gas. It must be taken in by their roots in chemical forms called nitrates. Here microbes are very, very important. Ammonia joins with other chemicals in the earth to form ammonium salts. Then,

through the activities of two kinds of bacteria, the nitrogen in the ammonium is changed to nitrates which plants can use.

Still other bacteria change nitrogen in the air of the soil to substances plants can take in. Some of these bacteria live freely in the soil, but others enter the roots of plants such as beans, peas, clover, and alfalfa. There they form colonies that look like little lumps on the roots. The microbes in the colonies take their food from the plants in which they live. But at the same time they trap nitrogen in the air of the soil and make it into substances that the plant uses. Even after the plants are harvested their roots full of nitrogen substances enrich the soil. Farmers often plant alfalfa or clover, then plow it under to fertilize their fields with the nitrogen products that bacteria have made.

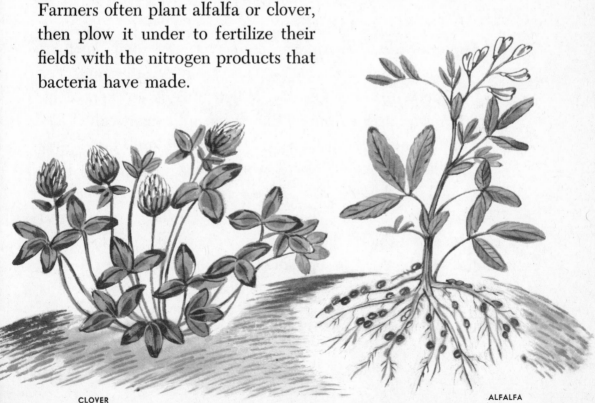

CLOVER   ALFALFA

SOME OF YOUR FOODS

Microbes also help make some everyday foods such as cheese, sauerkraut, and pickles. They are especially important to the cheese-making industry. When milk is not kept cold, certain bacteria in it change the sweet milk sugar called lactose into an acid called lactic acid. Then the milk tastes sour and smells bad. As the bacteria in it keep multiplying, they make more and more acid and the milk curdles. It separates into two layers: a thin watery portion, or whey, that rises to the top; and a thick solid substance, or curd, that settles at the bottom. If the curd is separated from the whey and pressed, cheese is made. Cottage cheese is plain curd; cream cheese is curd with a little sweet cream added.

All the other cheeses are made from curd, too. They have various flavors and various degrees of hardness because cheese manufacturers add to curd a particular kind of microbe for each kind of cheese—a microbe that the manufacturers know will make the cheese they want. The chemicals produced by each kind of microbe makes the differences in cheeses. In Swiss cheese they even make the holes! The microbes for Swiss cheese are added to cows' milk curd which is pressed into large blocks. Then these large blocks of cheese are put into dark cellars where the temperature is just right for the microbes to start multiplying. As they take in food they break down certain substances in the cheese and give off a great deal of waste gas. The gas cannot escape through the thick curd, so it forms little pockets inside of the cheese. These pockets are the holes that are in Swiss cheese.

Nowadays, cheese makers know exactly which microbes will produce each kind of cheese and can buy the ones they need to manufacture a particular type.

In making butter, also, the cream is sometimes allowed to sour slightly before it is churned. Microbes sour it just as they sour milk.

Sauerkraut is another food produced by microbes. In making it, cabbage is cut up into fine pieces and salt is added. The salt draws out the sweet juices from the cabbage. Then microbes that naturally live on the cabbage and in the air change the sugar of the juices into acid. The acid gives the sour taste of sauerkraut.

Cucumbers placed in salt water and spices become pickles because of microbes. The salt water draws the sugars from the cucumbers. Then microbes gradually change the sugars to acid. The acid seeps into the cucumbers and replaces the air in their cells. They turn sour and lose their green color. That is, they become pickles.

Microbes make vinegar from fruit juices or grain sugars. Certain yeasts ferment the sweet juices into alcohol. Then bacteria change the alcohol to acetic acid, which gives vinegar its sour taste. Vinegar made from fermented apple juice is called cider vinegar; that made from fermented grape juice is called wine vinegar; and that made from the fermented sugars of barley malt or other cereals to which malt is added is called malt vinegar.

So, microbes are important in making some of our foods. More than that, they themselves can be used as food. Scientists have found that these tiny plants and animals contain as much protein by weight as beefsteak does. Even today, many people in Japan, Ireland, and other countries eat algae in the form of seaweed as a vegetable. Scientists are experimenting with microbes to see if in the future they may furnish a good supply of food.

MICROBES AND THE WORK OF THE WORLD

Microbes are helpful in other ways besides food making, drug making, and enriching the soil. Many industries in all parts of the world use microscopic plants and animals in making various products.

Microbes, for example, were formerly used widely in the making of linen thread and hemp rope. Both of these products are manufactured from plant fibers—long, threadlike parts of the plants. Linen is made from flax; hemp rope from the hemp plant. When these plants are alive, the fibers are very tightly held together with a tough gluey material called pectin. This natural glue must be dissolved before the fibers can be separated and used. Here microbes can help. After the plants are cut down, if they are soaked in water, microbes immediately start using the pectin as food and so destroy its gluey form. The fibers can then be separated and made into linen and rope. Not all manufacturers now use this natural method of separating the fibers, but it is still employed in many countries.

Formerly microbes were widely used in the leather industry. They decayed or ate away all the dead flesh and hairs that stuck to hides, and left them clean and workable, ready to be tanned into leather. Although most large industries now use chemicals to clean the hides, this old natural method is still used in some countries.

Microbes help the coffee and cocoa industries. Since only the beans of the cocoa and coffee plants are useful, the fleshy pulp which surrounds these beans must be removed. Microbes decay the pulp, so cleaning it away.

THE HARMFUL MICROBES

In addition to the many, many helpful microbes there are harmful ones—the disease germs. These are the microbes that in the past have changed history by weakening armies and almost destroying whole cities full of people. They still cause much illness today, although we now understand how to control many of them.

Disease germs are much like all other microbes. Helpful and harmful microbes look much alike and they grow in much the same way. All of them are merely living their natural lives without any aim of being helpful or harmful. But some of them naturally attach themselves to plants, animals, or human beings and cause harm while they grow and multiply. They are the disease germs, and they are usually parasites. When they enter the body they grow very quickly by feeding on blood and tissue fluids. Then they cause a breakdown in the normal workings of the body and illness results.

Luckily our bodies have defenses to protect us against germs. Most of the germs that are swallowed are destroyed by the acids in the stomach. Most of those that we breathe into our lungs are coughed up. Microbes that enter a cut may start pushing their way into the deeper tissues. There they grow and multiply. The body immediately brings up its defenses. First, certain cells in the body line up and try to surround the microbes. They

55

form a wall to keep the germs from going farther. Other cells in the body called *phagocytes* (FAG-o-sites) can destroy germs. These special cells rush to the wounded area and start cleaning away the harmful microbes. Usually these phagocytes keep the germs from spreading, and the disease or infection is stopped.

If there are a great many germs, however, or if they are especially strong, they break through this first line of defense and spread through the body. Once this happens, a person becomes ill.

The body's last line of defense rallies when everything else has failed to stop microbes. Certain cells in the body can form special materials called *antibodies,* which work against germs. In various ways they stop the invading germs or make them harmless. Antibodies protect you. If you have these special substances in your body you will be able to resist various diseases.

MOLDLIKE ACTINOMYCETES WHICH CAUSE DISEASE

By inoculation a doctor can inject antibodies into a person to help him fight some diseases. A doctor can also help a person's body to produce antibodies by giving him a vaccine. Vaccines are merely weakened or dead microbes of certain diseases, in a solution. When this solution is introduced into a person's body, antibodies are produced to fight these microbes. If enough antibodies are made, they will protect the person when he comes accidentally in contact with more of these same disease microbes. Probably almost everyone has been inoculated with smallpox vaccine. The little mark on his arm or leg shows that he has built up antibodies against smallpox microbes. Because he has these substances in his body he is protected from these microbes.

FIGHTING HARMFUL MICROBES

Destroying harmful microbes is very important, and killing microbes that cause disease and spoilage is an everyday activity. There are many ways to do this.

Microbes need food and water in order to be active and multiply. If they do not have these things many of them will die and the others will become inactive. Keep food in cool dry places where microbes cannot grow easily.

Many microbes are killed by sunlight. The natural action of sunlight destroys some of them in the air and also destroys many microbes on things exposed to the sun's rays.

Microbes are strongly affected by changes in temperature. Strong heat is one of the best means of killing harmful microbes. They are destroyed by burning, boiling, baking, or steaming. Every day these methods are used. Milk is pasteurized; we burn waste materials; Mother steams the baby's bottles. In hospitals, instruments are steamed before an operation; linens are boiled; bandages and dressings are heated so that microbes on these materials will be destroyed.

Microbes can be killed by some chemicals, called antiseptics or germicides. In the treatment of cuts and other wounds it is important to apply a chemical such as iodine, mercurochrome, or alcohol after the cut is cleaned.

Microbes in the air can be killed by spraying certain chemicals in fine mists. Microbes on the floor can be destroyed by adding disinfectant chemicals to the scrub water. When you wash your hands with soap you remove not only dirt but many, many microbes.

Cleanliness is one of the best ways of fighting harmful microbes. Good health is another way. A healthy body, kept in good condition by plenty of healthful food, is able to protect itself well against harmful microbes.

FAMOUS WORKERS WITH MICROBES

Before the time of Lazaro Spallanzani, an eighteenth-century Italian scientist, no one was certain how microbes started. Most people believed that they developed accidentally, without any parents. But Spallanzani said, "Nonsense! They *must* have parents!" In 1768, by showing that microbes did not develop in broth which was boiled a long time and then tightly sealed, he showed that they really did come from other microbes of the same kind.

Edward Jenner, an English physician, was the discoverer of vaccination. In 1796 he inoculated a boy with matter taken from a sore on the hand of a dairymaid who had milked cows infected with cowpox, a disease of cows that resembles smallpox. Later, when Dr. Jenner inoculated the same boy for smallpox, he was not ill. This experiment called physicians' attention to vaccination, and later our modern methods were perfected.

Theodor Schwann was a German physiologist who did very valuable work in the 1830's to show how microbes influence fermentation and decay. He also showed that yeast was a living organism. Both Louis Pasteur and Joseph Lister owed much to Schwann's experimental work.

Joseph Lister, an English surgeon, first experimented with making surgery germfree in 1865, when he applied carbolic acid to surgical wounds to kill harmful microbes. Gradually he perfected his methods and today, owing to his pioneer work, surgical operations are antiseptic.

In 1876 Robert Koch, a poor, modest doctor in a German village, was the first man to discover that one particular kind of microbe causes one definite disease. Working alone in his home he found the microbe that causes anthrax, an animal disease that killed thousands of cattle and sheep in Europe at that time. Later he discovered the bacillus that causes tuberculosis. He also learned how to grow pure colonies of one particular kind of microbe on various solid foods—a process that was very valuable to experimenters.

In 1944 Selman A. Waksman of Rutgers University discovered streptomycin, an antibiotic. For years he had been studying microbes of the soil, and in 1939 he realized that some of these might be valuable in making modern drugs. He and his co-workers made over 10,000 microbe cultures from soil samples. From their experiments came streptomycin, useful in fighting many body infections.

THE MIGHTY MICROBES

Every day, scientists learn more about making use of the helpful microbes and controlling the harmful ones. More than ever before, microbes are playing an important part in our lives.

In recent years, scientists have found that these tiny bits of living matter contain important clews to how our own bodies work. By studying the chemical processes by which simple molds and bacteria carry on life, scientists have found some valuable hints about how all living things are able to exist. By observing microbes they have also gained some knowledge of how vitamins work and how the human body protects itself against disease. Scientists say that microbes are real storehouses of information which, in time, may help them solve more of the mysteries of living.

Microbes are truly amazing. Silently and invisibly they carry on their lives. And in so doing they perform services for every one of us. For microbes play an important part in the life of the earth. They make it possible for plants to grow; they keep refuse cleared away; they help in making some of our foods; they produce the chemicals for the wonder drugs that have saved countless lives. And scientists expect to find in the future that they perform other miracles. Truly the microbes are small but mighty.

GLOSSARY

algae (AL-jee)—a group of plants without leaves, roots, or stems, some of which contain chlorophyll. Some species are single microscopic cells. A single one is called an *alga*.

amoeba (a-MEE-ba)—a species of simple one-celled animal that constantly changes its shape and moves by means of finger-like projections

antibiotics (AN-ti-by-OTT-iks)—chemical substances, naturally produced by microbes, which act against other microbes

antibodies (AN-ti-bod-eez)—substances existing or developed in the body which act against poisons produced by microbes or destroy the microbes

bacilli (ba-SILL-eye)—rod-shaped bacteria

bacteria (bac-TEER-i-a)—a group of one-celled plant microbes which have no definite nucleus. A single one is called a *bacterium*.

budding—the process by which most new yeast cells form

buds—small bumps on the sides of yeast cells—the beginning of new yeast plants

cells (sells)—the small units of protoplasm of which living plants and animals are made

chlorophyll (KLO-ro-fil)—the green coloring matter of plants which is necessary for the forming of plant foods in the leaves or cells

cilia (SILL-i-a)—tiny hairlike threads which extend from certain microbes. These threads move back and forth and make the microbes move.

cocci (KOK-seye)—round bacteria

colony—a group of microbes of one species growing closely together

cyst (sist)—the resting stage of certain protozoa

fermentation—the process by which certain microbes naturally break down sugars into other chemicals

flagella (fla-JEL-la)—long whiplike threads that extend from some plant or animal microbes. Lashed back and forth, these make the microbes move. A single one is called a *flagellum*.

fungi (FUN-ji)—a group of plants made up of molds, mildews, rusts, smuts, mushrooms, toadstools, and similar forms. They are parasites or saprophytes. A single one is called a *fungus*.

63

genus (JEE-nus)—a group of related plant or animal species

membrane (MEM-brane)—the thin outer covering of a cell

micro-organism (MIKE-ro-OR-gan-izm)—a plant or animal so small that it can be seen only with the aid of a microscope

mold—a group of plant microbes most of which live on dead plant or animal matter. They often form a tangled web of long threads.

nucleus (NU-cle-us)—a thick mass in the protoplasm of most plant and animal cells—the part thought to be responsible for their growth and reproduction. The name for more than one nucleus is *nuclei* (NU-clee-eye).

Paramecium (par-a-MEE-shi-um)—a slipper-shaped animal micro-organism that moves by means of cilia

parasite (PAR-a-site)—a plant or animal that lives on, and obtains food from, some other living plant or animal

pasteurization—a process of heating a liquid in order to destroy harmful microbes

phagocytes (FAG-o-sites)—cells in the body, the special activity of which is to destroy disease microbes

protoplasm (PRO-to-plazm)—the jelly-like inner material of cells—a substance with the mysterious quality of being alive.

protozoa (pro-to-ZO-a)—single-celled animals—the lowest form of animal life

saprophyte (SAP-ro-fite)—a plant or animal that lives on dead or decaying plant or animal matter

species (SPEE-sheez)—a single kind of plants or animals having features in common that distinguish them from all other living things

spirilla (spy-RILL-a)—spiral-shaped bacteria

vaccine (VACK-seen)—a material which, when introduced into the body, stimulates it to form antibodies. Vaccines may be made of dead microbes or their products, or of living weakened microbes, in a solution.

vacuoles (VACK-u-oles)—small food-storage spaces in the protoplasm of certain microbes

yeasts—a group of plant microbes which reproduce by means of budding, and which cause fermentation

64

INDEX

alfalfa 49
algae 32-33, 52
ammonia 48
amoeba 22-23, 26
animal microbes 9, 22, 24-31
Anopheles mosquito 30
anthrax 13, 61
antibiotics 36-37, 61
antibodies 56-57
antiseptics 58-59, 61
bacilli 42-43, 61
bacteria 10-11, 41-45, 49, 50, 62
beans 49
bread mold 34-35
breadmaking 39-40
breathing 18
budding 38
butter 51
carbon dioxide 18, 32, 39-40, 48
cells 6-8, 43-44, 55-56
cheese 12, 36, 50-51
chlorophyll 23, 32, 34
cilia 28
cleanliness 59
clover 49
cocci 41-42
cocoa 54
coffee 54
colonies 14-15, 34, 44, 49, 61
cyst 26
decay 16-17, 18, 19, 47-48, 54, 60
disease microbes 16, 27, 30, 34, 36-37, 42, 45, 55-59, 60-61

disinfectants 58-59
false feet 22-23, 26
fermentation 12, 39-40, 52, 60
flagella 27, 42-43
flax 53-54
Fleming, Alexander 36
food for microbes 16-17, 21-23, 25, 26, 27, 28, 32, 39, 48
foods 4, 39-40, 50-52
fungi 34
genus 14
germicides 58-59
germs 4, 55-59; see also Disease microbes
glossary 63-64
hemp 53-54
inoculation 57
Jenner, Edward 60
Koch, Robert 61
laboratories 19-20
leather 4, 54
Leeuwenhoek, Anton van 10-11
Lister, Joseph 60, 61
malaria 30
membrane, cell 7, 21-22, 23
micro-organisms 3
microscopes 3, 5, 11
mildews 34
milk 13, 50-51, 58
molds 19, 34-37, 62
nitrates 48-49
nitrogen 18, 48-49
nucleus 8, 25, 31, 45
oxygen 8, 18, 33
Paramecium 28, 29

parasites 16, 30, 34, 45, 55
Pasteur, Louis 12-13, 60
pasteurization 13, 58
peas 49
penicillin 36-37
phagocytes 56
pickles 52
plant microbes 9, 21-23, 32-45
plants 8, 46-49
protoplasm 7
protozoa 24-31; see also Animal microbes
reproduction 30, 31, 35, 38-39, 43-44
saprophytes 16
sauerkraut 51-52
Schwann, Theodor 60
size of microbes 2, 14
smallpox 57, 60
soil microbes 46-49, 61
Spallanzani, Lazaro 60
species 14
spirilla 43
spores 35
streptomycin 37, 61
sunlight 19, 58
temperature 18, 51, 58
terramycin 37
tuberculosis 61
vaccination 13, 57, 60
vacuoles 23, 25, 26, 28
vinegar 52
viruses 45
Volvox perglobator 14-15
Waksman, Selman A. 61
water 17, 32, 33, 58
yeasts 38-40, 60

65

MICROBES (GREATLY ENLARGED)

Date Due

DEMCO NO. 294

MAY 4	Brian Cydus			
JUN 5				
MAY OCT 9 '70	Cosgen			
FEB 7 '72	MARK Delfine			
	Heinrick			